AF624614

The Weird Times

(But They Weren't That Hard)

Kilcon Neatoe

BookLeaf Publishing

Presentation by *BookLeaf Publishing*

Web: www.bookleafpub.com

E-mail: info@bookleafpub.com

ISBN: 9789357212953

First edition 2023

ACKNOWLEDGEMENT

I want to acknowledge Kimberly Estes for helping me with "Connections (Drive Safely)" and Emily Elam for "Comfort" and "Comfort II".

COMFORT I

(Watch for the storks)

Then you felt secure,
At the places you were then -
When it wasn't this

With no thoughts those days,
In the nights we were awake -
Until we sacked out

We were unknowing,
Back before the kids evolved -
The paint dried slower

When it wasn’t this,
We’d do anything out there -
Then we chased shoebills

Later, they sped up,
And pushed us into a wall -
To the cold water

Then we saw new seas,
To chase new cities out there -
We kept the sea shells

Looking into those years,
I have comfort in you -
We were still there

CONNECTIONS

(Drive Safely)

The slow drives at night...
... drank away the dripped oceans
When you were shielded.

 It could change one day -

Think, "it was like that back then"
It would be real life.

So don't waste your breath -
The storks fly from your movement
You'll drive until death.

When the time gets old -
And the moments shrink away
There's only then, right?

Find what makes you drive -
And then you'll love the future
The past brought new times.

We tried to shrink it -
But the age wears like sandstone
Slow the formation.

You'll go and achieve -
And cruise against the stop signs
Or they'll take your car.

I FOUND A BOX IN THE BASEMENT

A gift from someone left for the ages
Somehow survived a basement floor for months.
I opened a box and saw it folded -
A blanket sat under movies and books.

My chest ached and murmured when I saw it,
Trapped in a frozen wind that stunned my heart rate
In my head, the memories rode a boat -
They tipped in the water, floated, and flipped.

I found a disc in there on the blanket -
A 2000's movie about someone
Who learned to make better, healthy habits
The critics gave it a three-star rating.

I used to have a DVD player -
It drowned in the old, flooded basement dirt.
Then rusted and weathered to a relic -
Some disc fused to the slot inside of it.

I don't have that DVD player now -
I can't watch The Man In The Window.
The back only shows it's an odd thriller,
So I'll push the snow out of the sidewalk.

THE FLAMING SALVOS

(The Journey Changed For Life)

I wrapped in sheets and attested to
The memories of days that fell asleep.
Oh, he smashed batteries to slime
And asked if he could eat a black
millipede.

I sagged in the pew, tearing behind
shades.
He lied in the casket, now gone,
asleep.
The salvos of thoughts I usually
scathed -
Turned to others to shoot and rain.

He was a boy being who he was:
He was a (rough) playful, (blunt)
honest boy
With nothing to say, his father's face
soaked.
Then his mother watched his son lie
there dead

I wrapped in sheets and attested to
The knowledge that hit me later than
it should
Starting with a whine, then a scream,
my throat shut
...

HOW MUSICIANS DEAL WITH FEELINGS

(More music)

He came to life with music
And so did his sister those days
On chilled, streamlined highways those nights,
With streaks that would never stop.

He stayed out later than she thought
Then he went to the double bars.
Like a flower pressed in a book,
He turned fluffy and preserved.

She belted that last shivering performance
Whether five or sixty-five, the months were obsolete
Five or sixty-five, he was there,
And five or sixty-five, not.

The young man's guitar stayed in the corner
His piano gathered much more, more dust
His pictures hung on the walls,
And she drove back to Boston.

Her brain sliced her heart strings, but she lived on
Still, she learned at the end of all the turmoil...

...There was nothing left - she learned nothing new.
There was only music to help her think.

She came to life with music,
And so did everyone those days.
In colorful light bulbs, she grew
She sang songs so she could breathe.

RANSACKING THE BASEMENT

I ransacked the basement, until the
ground fell to pieces
The dusty boxes were soiled with mildew
and dry fumes
The years of isolation gave the air
breathed wrinkles
But it's here, and it's cleared to the
point that I can see the floor.

The books I've never wanted to read sat on
the tall shelf
Soiled stuffed dolls rotted together on
the rocky floor
I waded my feet through the tripping
hazards below me,
Then uncovered the windows, turned off
the light, and fled out.

IN THE ATTIC

Climbing up the ladder, I pushed up the board
A city of cobwebs landed on my body
They entered my lungs, then dissolved away
And that is how discovering a new world goes for you

You're left to your own devices somewhere
With creaking boards and soft spots on your feet
They bend and snap as you tread over cracks
You learn how to walk around the old attic

Lifting out the boxes was tougher for me to pull off
Why do people try too hard, or at all?
Maybe, the finished image is worth more than the longer job,

But I can't agree with myself.

THE INTRO

In between the basement and attic was the house. Wide doors were shrugged like Atlas straining to hold the walls. The living room had a fritzing TV.

I found a new DVD player in the attic, and its height saved its life. I fixed the old TV and it went.

The movie looked great. The movie played. It was a simple program, skipping to the start. The man's lights were off and his kitchen light lit the house, in those sets that were meant to look plastic and perfect.

He walked out of the house and into the woods. Then he slipped into the mud and landed in a cave. In the cave, he found an exit to the outside world. Then he went about his day.

He returned to his house, late at night. Then he heard footsteps in the absence of the light. The dog jumped on the bed to go to sleep. Then he went on with his life.

THE MAN IN THE WINDOW

He watched from behind the flowered curtains
And stalked the figure that stood by the tree
He matched its snapped pace as he locked the glass
And its hands pressed on the weak, fiber screen
"You'll have to change one day. You need to grow."
But to no avail, the monster walked
The man lit the room and made his loud noise

A month later, the sky had fallen down
He waited by the carpet on his burned knees
The form encroached to him and ripped the screen
Its breath pressed on the cold, wet, solid glass
"You'll have to –"."
He closed the blinds, turned on the lights, played games

A year passed, then, the man woke up
early
The buzz from the distractions grazed his
bones
So he turned off the TV and light bulbs
The figure welcomed itself into the
bedroom
It blended with the early light
It vanished after leaving the window

COMFORT II

We left in the night,
Inside the car on the road,
Racing for the new.

Then went somewhere now -
to find a gift you can't find there,
I couldn't box it.

Our fears chased us down -
They tried to drag us back down,
But we fought them back

Ha ha, you were right -
I've always been too carefree,
Not looking ahead.

We fled the ocean -
Now, we aren't chasing shoebills,
We're finding new terrain...

...I used to think, well -
That lost belief wasn't true...
..."When it wasn't this."

The present is good,
And given the things I've seen,
Breath is currency.

The future improves,
And the past died in those graves,
Where there were no crows.

I used to say that -
Well, maybe I was just wrong,
Who said hope was crime?

Who said we were right?
We were trapped in the time
We couldn't stay there.

And then it was now -
Although it's all different,
You still have next time.

Don't mind my spiel -
I loved the road trip we had
I'll see you next month.

THREE MONTHS LATER

Sitting on the roof,
I tied myself to the house.
You wanted space there

The sun is falling
And the night is waking up.
I strive to go *back*

If there were a place
It would not be the past.
'Cause *back* would be you

Ha! The last three months
They've been faster than this one.
This week has been slow

Just in the best way
With all I could've asked for.
I can hear better

I love you, ha ha.
Is what I can only say -
To myself this time 'round.

THE PEACOCK

Dark blue dress shirts and banter about your new shoes
You have heels that make you a little taller
Traditional views about what people do
Blocks in how I perceive other people

On-white doors opened, wide for you, and shined
Like lights out of your odd, murky glasses
Covered fabric chairs stretched in lines near the floor
Where students and teachers dance, but not you

In the space in your mind, I'm the villain
My wants on both sides, second building to the right
Yet, here you are again, before me
You steal back the gifts you gave me that night

You confided in a stranger you hated
Thinking your thoughts would hit the mirror and bounce
You said these were weird times, but you loved them
Why else did you embrace every moment?

That's what they said
Little did they know...
... that I knew what they didn't,
When they left in defeat.

THE RESTAURANT

Under a red sky and a chilly night
The restaurant was bustling with people
Inside, the walls were pre-cut and
unscathed
In white walls and dark-wooden boards

The kids screamed to their seats, as a few
people sauntered out
Nothing new was here today
But underneath the building was a chest

There was no way to access it, but the
owner tried
He pulled apart the boards until the
flooring was gone
And inside the box was browned
newspaper
Wrapped around old rusted glass and
picture frames

The pictures of a family he didn't know
lived in the basement
So he stored them away on the store's
walls
"Who are they?" They'd ask.
"I'm not sure. I found them downstairs."
The owner then said.

"They made nice decorations for the place." He shrugged.
"I didn't even have to buy any frames."
The grasses in the photos were shadowed
The figure shoveling the snow was ready to sleep

Then I went to the frames and asked myself,
"Why is there such a semblance?"
"I need to modernize."
I ran past the ocean of cars and left.

YELLOW CAT I

There's fire, spice, burn, and age
The colors on the painting change
The cat thought of what a person is

The string was tangled, the fridge was
chilled with ice
All that's there was a pair of eyes
They're tall cats with no whiskers

There's a stove of food she pawed to
She meowed through the door
How did they make doors?

She hung off the cliff and stared at the
floor
She sat on a couch and sprawled
Maybe they were always there?

She went to the basement and jumped in a
box
The cold from the ground poured into her
feet
She landed in a box and went to sleep

There's ice, dust, freeze, and immortality
Sometimes nothing needs to happen
For you to be happy

YELLOW CAT II

Engrossing shadows held the basement. The cat stretched and strutted from their torsos. Twitching her tail, she made her way to the kitchen, and knocked the plate of chicken to the floor. She sat on the cliff over the ravine.

JUST CROWS AND ROBINS

Robins and crows fly over the old graves. A soft moss grows over the stone hedges. They're only there for food or to sit down. Birds don't care as to why humans placed stones.

They stomp on the stones and would continue, if they knew why we built walls around them. Their world flows up and down slower than ours, and they're notorious for wanting bread.

A long concrete sea separates the yards. The seals and sharks stop to let me cross it. The leaves crunch under my feet into the air, then the spirits in the background drop.

They subside and let me visit them there, while watching from a near distance to me. There's a closing shuffle in the leaves. I tread to the benches seated on the ground.

The gravel path bends inside the hills where no crows nor robins visited there. They'd rather be somewhere cleaner to visit the more refined places.

An ageless five-foot bird gleams in the shade. It blinks through the trees in a far-sighted view, and with its scraping beak and tiny legs, it rocks. Then it struts away, leaving a breeze.

In the blanket, I attested to something - The long ambiguity. I know I can get out, it will happen. I can go through everything I'll face.

THE STUDIO

Bright glowing lights on the rail in the night
Two on the zip ties, five on the inside
Industrial strips fused to the concrete
Blocks making the sidewalk break into gravel

On-white doors bolted, locked over, and shut
Lights stretch into the front of the three walls
Solid metal chairs by the water and rocks
And fish and tiny tables by the wall

At the space in other places sat the
Cars on both sides, second building to the right
Waiting for the party, right before the class
At the corner of the street is the studio

THE MAN IN THE WINDOW II

(The End Of The Movie)

The lights were off, and the sounds were silenced The shadow chewed the glass, as its breath fogged
He opened it -
He ran to it

And then the darkness crept inside the room
with its tongue dangling and its claws bright
It stalked his moves -
He grew rigid.

The room was cold where he was on his own
He flipped on the switch and the monster said
"You made your own" -
His joy returned.

"3.2 / 5 stars" "Straight to DVD"

Why do people try too hard, or at all? It's because we tickle our egos with what we think we could do, so we find what we're capable of. Why does it take so long? I want it in a second. I'm ready.

www.ingramcontent.com/pod-product-compliance
Lightning Source LLC
Chambersburg PA
CBHW062111140826
49812CB00058B/1247
9789357212953